BURNT OFFERINGS

Parables for 20th-Century Christians

ELVIN T. EBERHART

ABINGDON • NASHVILLE

BURNT OFFERINGS

Library of Congress Cataloging in Publication Data

Eberhart, Elvin T. 1925–
  Burnt offerings.
  1. Parables. I. Title.
BV4515.2.E23   248'.4   77-23158

ISBN 0-687-04375-1

To all the people who are trying to live the best way they know how. Without the likes of them these tales could never have been written.

Contents

Introduction

When the editors suggested that I might write an introduction, I recalled a cartoon I'd seen years back. A barber was holding a mirror to the back of his customer's head so that the customer could see his haircut from behind. The caption read: "Never mind the mirror! What's done is done!"

These Burnt Offerings were collected from a weekly publication I write for the patients in Salem Hospital. While there is some disagreement on the matter, I don't feel you have to be ill to read them. They were written for people who are busy living out their personal lives. The sickroom provided me with a captive audience—an opportunity no clergyman ever resists.

This is a collection. So dip in and read as you will at the pace you choose. It is not a cover-to-cover book to be read in one sitting.

My intent in these writings was to express humor in a form that is accepting of life rather than being critical or condemning of it. Whatever success I've had in achieving this goal I owe to Will Rogers, who showed me that significant thoughts can be expressed humorously; Robert Benchley, who showed me that there's laughter in our pretentions; O. Henry, who showed me the delight in surprise endings; and George Ade, who showed me how to bring it all together.

I deeply appreciate the courage of Irwin Wedel and Peter Sukalac of Salem Hospital in allowing me to push my wares onto the patients. Also, my undying thanks goes to my wife, Persis, who did all the boring work in getting this material ready for the printer, and who gave me much good counsel and advice even when I didn't want it. Somehow she did all of this and kept the family going, too.

Elvin T. Eberhart

The Playboy Who Had to Live with His Past

But when he came to himself he said, "How many of my father's hired servants have bread enough and to spare, but I perish here with hunger!"

—Luke 15:17

Once a certain man had two sons, and one took his education in cash and went to the wild-oats country as a free-and-easy.

He got in solid with those who hadn't learned that money could not buy happiness. They showed him the kind of living best sellers are made of. In appreciation he threw wide his vault, and a good time was had by all.

His brother was solid citizen who developed his potentials on a cap-and-gown tour. He learned about debit and credit and what happens by playing fast and loose with economic principles. Then he returned to the family hardware business and took his place behind the calculator.

He had his money at 8 percent, paid all bills promptly, and supported the school budget. As a public service, he lectured on "How to Keep a Good Credit Rating," updating his jokes each year to show he was abreast of the times.

Meanwhile, the unimproved variety reaped his harvest. He was sloshing along the bottom of the barrel and would not turn down a dime from a stranger. Then he came to himself and said, "My father's hired help have bread enough and to spare, but I perish here with hunger! I'll go home and work as janitor."

But his father took one look at him, tore up his application, and made him a junior partner. The down-and-outer was as astonished as was the solid citizen who wanted a how-come that brother made starting lineup while missing spring training.

"Because I'm coaching," said Dad. "Besides, acts like this

give fatherhood a good name. Now teach him what a partner should know.''

The prodigal was grateful. He was ready to apply himself and spend his nights reading hardware literature. But before he could forget his past he was buttonholed to give the Men's Monday Lunch Club a personalized glimpse of depravity in exchange for a roast beef plate with dessert.

He said he would, and he did.

He came right to the point with mine-was-a-misspent-youth theme, documenting his opinion with picturesque illustrations which caused his audience not to lose interest.

The life of thrills was dead end, he said. This shocking revelation came to him one cold evening while doing the panhandler bit. Right then he saw that the real life was to be more like his brother who had it in spades. Now if they would excuse him, he had to get back to work.

It was standing ovation!

Word of his splendid message spread. He spoke at service clubs, churches, and schools. All who heard him knew that only disgrace and ruin lay ahead for any who tried to live such as he had.

His popularity grew until he was on the lecture tour at $2,000 per. The day he sold the movie rights of his life story for an undisclosed sum, his brother received a gold-plated pin honoring his fifteen years as treasurer of the Young Campers of the Trail.

Thought for the day: *It's the beginning that counts.*

The Braggart
Who Was Put to the Test

*Your light must shine before people, so that they will see
the good things you do.*
                                        —*Matthew 5:16*a *(TEV)*

There was once a certain man who specialized in big talk, so
wherever he went he was known as all wind and no show, which
was an accurate description. Being so advised did not bother him
for deep down he knew he was first-class merchandise fully
guaranteed to produce as advertised. On occasions when he had
self-doubt he needed only to twirl the ends of his wax-tipped
mustache for reassurance.

Now he came by way of the big city to a small town going
straight to the office of the local *Weekly Herald* where he was
immediately made editor—his mother being the publisher and in
need of any help she could get, paid circulation being what it
was.

With his help and direction, word around town had it that he
knew his stuff working on the big city papers as he had. For
proof one had only to glance through his trunkload of plaudits
and awards which right now were in storage. His alert mind was
already working out a prize-winning editorial for the *Herald*. Of
course, final copy would have to wait until he had a proper feel
of the town which would, naturally, take some time.

Being of the exceptional sort he'd topped the ladder in several
other fields as well. These he willingly scenarioed to any crowd
of one or more. Once, hearing that a local church needed a choir
director reminded him of his several musical distinctions in
guest conducting outstanding choral groups in cities here and
there.

Now all of this gave him a large following of scoffers and

disbelievers who wanted to shove him into a put-up-or-shut-up. Now they saw their chance with the choir and moved in and made ready for the execution.

Such talent as yours, they said, should not be hidden but must shine before people so that they can see the good things you do. Why not throw the switch tonight at choir rehearsal.

He OK'd the invite with a twirl of the mustache, and immediately the town odds favored him in doing a no show. Nevertheless, it was standing room only in the choir loft that night.

He was true to his word. At the appointed time he center-aisled it straight to the organist, asking for copies of the choir's current repertoire. A hushed silence fell as he studied the music twirling his mustache methodically.

Then the moment of truth! He looked up saying right out loud in front of God and everybody that their level of performance was so far below his attainments in directing that there was no possibility of working together.

With that he left without so much as a blush.

Thought for the day: *A teller of tales does not neglect the ending.*

The Preacher Who Got It the Hard Way

All things work together for good.
—Romans 8:28b (ASV)

There was once a certain preacher who hung up his shepherd's crook each Monday and went to the green pastures with a bright red cap, spiked shoes, and a set of clubs. Golf was his principal weakness—a matter he tried correcting at every opportunity, his score being what it was.

His only contact with par was by way of theory. He played with the faith of Abraham, teeing off not knowing whither he was going. His way to the green was through uncharted territory, and his chip shots were sure things to cross the green to the other side. And his putting was the back-and-forth method.

Still there was no known cure for his kind of fever—a fact obvious to his congregation. He oft told them that golf was really a game of life. "You have to play the ball where it lays," he said; and, "Even from a poor start there's a chance for recovery. Those who know the game can better understand St. Paul who tried to go one direction but ended up going in another."

The people did say, "Surely the Lord is in this game and we did not know it." So the ladies' circle gave him a dozen new balls for his happy natal day. This pleased him greatly.

It was really too bad that tending his flock like he did left so little time to put the squeeze on par. But finally came that day of days when it was his turn to reap the rewards of a well-done-good-and-faithful servant. Which meant a monthly pay-off from his pension board and a low handicap.

He became a regular sight at the course. Through devotion and perseverance his drives fell onto smooth places, his approaches were dandies which added up to scores with respectability.

In this new life he kept company with a class of men who were not getting younger. Like them he took a couple of time-outs for a heart tune-up. But each time he got back into the swing with no sign of lost ground.

One summer day while the dew was still on the roses he took his stance at the first tee with that all-right feeling. He slammed a wow-look-at-that drive, cozied a five iron next to the pin, and did a sure putt to start par on the run.

It was his day. He kept chasing par right through the fifteenth hole when he got a familiar feeling in his chest and down his arm. Right away he knew it was a message from the heart. This was a first-order blow to have happen on this kind of round. While pondering what to do he remembered that the next three holes lay in the direction of the club house. He could play them out and go in at the same time. Which he did.

Soon someone mistook his chest for a trampoline and started practice. This shortened his backswing but kept his head down. He still hit the ball. By the time he reached the eighteenth the guy on his chest had found a partner, and they were doing a doubles routine.

He tried not to feel it as he lined up his thirty-foot putt. He stood there a long time, perspiration on his head. Then he slowly stroked the ball just as the sun went black. When it turned yellow again he was lying on the green breathing through an oxygen mask. He looked at his partner, questioning. "You made it. Birdie four."

"Thank God!" he said. "A par round at last!"

Thought for the day: *A goal makes the difference.*

The Fledgling Pastor
Who Did as Well as Could Be Expected

I was sick and you visited me.
—Matthew 25:36b

A newest member in the ranks of the ordained got a nervous stomach whenever he thought of making a hospital call. In seminary he had sparred with spiritual comforting by way of approved textbooks. But now he was inside the ropes and expected to take on the real thing.

The closest he'd ever come to experiencing pain was a penicillin shot; and in the art of binding up wounds it was Band-Aids, iodine, and a kiss to make it well.

Nevertheless, there was a command burning inside him: "As you did it to one of the least of these my brethren, you did it to me." And his professor in Pastoral Care 256 Section B had told him of the unspeakable joys in being God's vessel.

So being a man of faith he swallowed hard and advised his flock that in their moments of pain and loneliness God's help was as near as the phone. He put his prayer book at the ready and waited for his moment of truth.

One evening, parishioner Johanson drove down the street and made an unexpected exit through the windshield, landing in the hospital's emergency room. His life was intact, but several bones needed realignment.

Hearing of the accident the young pastor grabbed his prayer book and, en route to the hospital, dress rehearsed several comforting thoughts designed for such occasions. He came through the rehearsal as a tower of spiritual strength and a conveyor of great compassion. It was opening night and he was ready.

Now his seminary books had neither pictures nor sound tracks, so what he was to see was a first for him. There stretched out with guy wires and pulleys like a repair job in a machine shop was Johanson. Tubes, needles, and gadgets protruded conspicuously from all over his body. His face was the color of sunset patterned with a black embroidery.

From the opening curtain it was stage fright. The pastor's mouth dried out; instead of his comforting thoughts he remembered he should be home preparing Sunday's sermon. His spirit fled. His body would have gone too except Mrs. Johanson was there watching.

A strange power held his tongue. He felt his pounding heart, the perspiration on his head, and his stomach shifting into reverse. Then the patient rolled his eyes, opened his mouth, and groaned something awful.

The symbol of God's presence cried, "Amen!" and fled.

Late the next morning he stumbled out of bed and went to the kitchen to tell his wife he was leaving the ministry. But before he could open his mouth, she told him that Mrs. Johanson had called and said how his visit had helped them greatly. They had gained composure through his quiet, sensitive mood and found strength for the night through his silent prayer.

Thought for the day: *Being an amateur is not always a handicap.*

The Man Whose Weekend Pilgrimages Were for Spiritual Reasons

And many peoples shall come, and say: "Come, let us go up to the mountain of the Lord . . . that he may teach us his ways and that we may walk in his paths."

—Isaiah 2:3 a

In a certain city where freeways and parking lots replaced peace and quiet there lived a devout man. From the days of his youth he had, without benefit of clergy, matured into a person whose place of worship was the great out-of-doors.

He was a true defender of the faith, saying, "I worship God in the high mountains. There I can feel his presence as nowhere else!"

Each week, weather permitting, he uniformed himself as a cross between a disaster area refugee and a boy scout drop-out taking pilgrimage into the high country where his beard worked on a two-day growth. Once freed from the fumes and noise of civilized life he covered himself with a mixture of mosquito repellent and camp smoke. He sat before his tent in the spirit of holiness while his children prepared wood for the altar fire, and his wife cooked the meals in approved fashion.

This free worshipper invited others of like persuasion to congregate with him. Together they philosophized about life and passed judgment on a has-been quarterback who signed a renewed contract for a figure with more zeros than they could count.

It was always a mountain-top experience. And he who had been in the divine presence returned to his eight-to-five saying, "I'm coming back to work only because I have to."

Such weekends gave him fireplace memories for the winter.

At which time he also read camp literature in preparation for the coming year.

Then in due season he said to his wife, "The winter is now gone. Come, let us go up to the mountain of the Lord that we may learn of his ways and that we may walk in his paths."

Preparation for the pilgrimage began. There was the tent to inspect, sleeping bags to air, camp stove and lantern to check, white gas to purchase, axe and knives to sharpen, menus to approve, food, ice, and proper beverages to buy.

When all was in readiness he said, "There will be many going to the mountains. Let us prepare for an early departure that we might have first choice of campsites."

"Well spoken, O devout one," said his wife.

And the next day, while the sun was yet high in the western sky, they found a likely spot within nature's cathedral. With experienced skill up went the tent, clothes lines, food box, camp chairs, and behold: A temple made with hands!

Having done all things needful, the devout one loosed his belt and stretched out on the portable chaise lounge for thirty minutes of silent meditation while the temple help prepared the sacrificial meal.

Thought for the day: *True worship requires careful thought and preparation.*

The Man with the How To
and What Happened When He Did

A man's mind plans his way,
but the Lord directs his steps.
—Proverbs 16:9

Once there was a young man whose specialty was making right choices and teaching others to do likewise.

He embarked on this career when he looked back over his twenty-seven years and saw he'd negotiated all of the forks in Life's Road. He gave himself a passing grade and then felt the humanitarian call to give his success secrets to other travelers for a slight consideration.

There was no doubting that he had a half nelson on uncertainty. He spoke as one having authority, who walked uprightly and signed his name in a big round hand.

His big start was with an adult education center where he had an inside room and two pieces of chalk. He was eager to develop a following, especially with the opposite sex, since he was yet single and desired to be otherwise. Soon local women's clubs booked him for twenty-five dollars plus seconds on punch and cookies.

When it was time for him to be stage center, he unfolded his solutions to the human predicament by telling of the two temptations lurking at the forks in the Road: To make camp and stay longer than the scenery warranted, and to try making up for lost time and rush on ignoring the signposts. Then he said, "Get the facts before the facts get you!"

He surrounded his splinter of wisdom with pauses so the people could tell it was important, and he polished it off into a pearl of great price, "Go to a quiet place, label each fact Pro or Con, but never Maybe; put them onto the proper side of the scale, and the right choice will flash on like the lights on a pinball machine."

Some who heard were stiff-necked people and asked for their money back. Others believed and wanted only to touch his hem.

While he was wondering when he'd find an altar mate, cupid hit him with two arrows right where it counted—one for the blonde with a red wig, a fun-and-games girl who traveled with intellectuals and the swells; the other for a blonde wearing a brunette wig, the pipe-and-slippers type with Sunday picnics in the park. The day came when the great decision maker had to choose, so he retired to the mountains for meditation and reflection.

In his solitude he saw as in a dream married life with each girl. He dog-tagged each fact and on the third day the scale tipped.

He gave thanks to the Great Matchmaker in the sky and hurried off to claim the red-headed blonde, only to learn that she'd done a ladder exit with an old college beau.

The master-of-his-own-fate made an unscheduled stop and confessed to the also-ran that he'd been thinking of her for three days. Would she do the cake-and-rice routine with him?

She said she would, and she did.

Thought for the day: *Circumstances make a difference.*

The Man Who Sailed with Progress and Where It Took Him

At the end of forty days Noah opened the window of the ark which he had made.

—*Genesis 8:6*

Once when the world was in a mess, the Lord decided to return to Go and start a new game. The only players were a boatload of animals and a proper family named Noah. All others withdrew due to heavy rains. In fact, it rained so much that there was nothing for them to do but drown—which they did.

This freed the Lord's hand so he could turn the world into a better place, which was what he had in mind all along. The Lord brought Noah into his extermination business because Noah was strictly gold star in doing the straight and narrow. However, Mrs. Noah did not think it a fitting profession for one so pure and righteous as her husband.

Noah told her that her idea was silly since what he was doing was for a good cause. "And what's more," he said, "progress is only possible if people sacrifice."

When he explained it like that, she said it all made sense. Then she shed a tear over being such a ninny and also over the thought of being locked up for months with wild animals in a dark ark.

So Noah showed her on the blueprints how the Lord had eliminated all trouble through advance design. He had planned a modern and up-to-date ark with space for family, animals, and food.

Now she didn't know anything about design, but she knew that cooping up wild animals was unnatural. Her woman's intuition told her trouble was dead ahead. Five days after the rains began Noah realized she had a point.

The food and animals were aboard, hatches battened down, oil lamps lit, and the Noahs were sitting around waiting for a better world. The animals lost their cool. They clawed, gnawed, and kicked in an irresponsible manner. Mrs. Noah's face took on an I-told-you-so look, and she dubbed the ark "The Lord's Folly."

Noah knew he'd built it to the Lord's specifications, so he could not account for the trouble. But the truth was that fresh air was in short supply.

Each new day of confinement was another day of misery and bedlam. The darkness seemed blacker, the lamps dimmer, the animals louder and more fierce. It was no longer safe to walk among them. And at times it seemed they might even devour one another.

After forty days the rains stopped and Noah opened the window. Seeing the clear sky, the crazed animals charged the bulkheads in an effort to break free. The ark rolled and creaked under the strain.

Right then Noah knew he'd had all the progress he wanted. The moment the land dried he threw open the door. The frenzied animals charged into the countryside disappearing over the hills.

Noah fell to the ground, planted a vineyard, and took to strong drink.

Thought for the day: *Air pollution is a difficult problem.*

The Two Men
Who Wanted to Reach the People

> *. . . imparting insight to the ignorant.*
> *—Proverbs 1:4a (Moffatt)*

Once there were two men who believed that the right way to live was in helping the other guy. Each decided to go at it by way of special education and training so as to do it right and proper.

One went to a school where English was a dead language. The school taught elocution in the form of eight-syllable words with a Latin ring. The man learned to give forth with all the expression of a plain brown wrapper. He studied hard for several years.

Then one day he answered all the right questions without once using common speech. His teachers did the tickled-pink and told him he was now on his own. They gave him his personal stethoscope, called him Doctor, and sent him into the world to help the other guy—which he did.

When his patients heard him speak, there was no doubt that he was pure medical wisdom and stature. But they did not know whether to feel good or bad after he told them how they were. So they made new appointments hoping to find out.

The other man went to a school which specialized in turning the simple into the complex. This meant learning to think differently from ordinary people. It was sure failure to allow horse sense and common logic to prejudice one's thinking. He learned that solutions were found by researching writings written so as to not be understood.

After some years he answered several questions designed to show that he was not like other people. When he demonstrated his proficiency in the art of confusion, they said he should be called Lawyer. They sent him into the world to help the other guy—which he did.

Clients came for help and counsel. He'd listen and right away let them know they were doing a sure tightrope. But he could save them from certain anguish by the use of his uncommon thinking. So they kept in close touch with him to be sure their simple ways did not lead to big trouble.

One day a mutual acquaintance of these two came to the lawyer saying the two should meet. The lawyer asked for a how-come. Right then the mutual acquaintance said awful things about the doctor. He was sure the doctor was not telling him all, which was causing him much worry and anguish. Well, the uncommon mind agreed that such a meeting might prove beneficial. He suggested they do it in his favorite hangout, a court of law.

On the appointed day all met in a courtroom presided over by a judge who had a golf game at 4:30. They also invited several others who did not know what was going on. Some would be on the jury. Now, as anyone knows, a jury is made up of common, ordinary folks. The more ignorant they are of the incidents involved, the better their qualifications. So according to the game rules the lawyers filled the jury with as ignorant a group of men and women as possible.

Now the rest of the time was spent in educating and imparting insights to the ignorant people as to what it was all about. To do this the doctor's words had to be put into street-corner language and the lawyer's uncommon thinking had to be done in an ignorant form. The judge called the foul, off-sides, net ball, roughing the kicker, and safe-at-second decisions. After a while the jurors went off to figure out what they'd learned.

Thought for the day: *Only important peoples' opinions really count.*

The Women's Club
That Planned for a Big Day

Let us not grow weary in well-doing.
*—Galatians 6:9*a

There was once a certain women's club that wanted to make the world a better place, which they did by way of meetings each Wednesday noon in a local eatery that had a back room with a swell name. Last year's world improvements, according to the treasurer, were worth $847.56, this being more than enough to produce approving nods from those whose opinions were It.

The club was a long-standing, complete with descriptive name, printed by-laws, board of directors duly elected, and three-year supply of blank checks with spaces for two signatures.

Still, all was not upward bound, it being noted that some were derelict in load-pulling, and more than a few were conspicuously absent from meetings. That was too bad since the mere price of a meal and annual dues of an agreed upon sum guaranteed them weekly programs of inestimable value.

However, some abstainers did put value on the inestimable and figured they were being shortchanged. Besides, the food wasn't all that great.

This became agenda item number one at the next board meeting—all members cordially invited.

Said meeting was *Robert's Rules of Order* as modified by local variances. After a goodly discussion was had by all, it was thumbs up on an "all in favor" to rally around Founders' Day with a program calculated to be unforgettable.

When translated, it meant a speaker with an attractive name would "for shame" those who were wearied in well-doing and recall them to sacrifice for the high principles of humanitarian service—all in uplifting words of course.

It so happened that such a one lived near by. They knew he'd do a drop everything when he got their invitation, being known the way they were and all. But just to make sure, the program chairwoman would lay it on thick. She did this by using their impressive letterhead.

She wrote that they were inviting him because his high caliber was a perfect match for their organization as anyone knew who examined the qualities of their service projects and their membership list. He was highly recommended as one whose message would inspire the club to renewed dedication, sacrificial service, as espoused in their club motto. And would he please reply as soon as possible to give ample time for their newspaper publicitiy to properly impress the community.

The attractive name answered, saying he was available. And since he, too, was dedicated to principles of service he would do a stellar attraction for his daytime minimum of three hundred dollars. Also, he would save them the price of a meal since he did not like to speak on a full stomach.

When the Founders' Day meeting was announced in the local paper, it was noted that the program, an historical review of the club's varied achievements, would be presented by one of its very own.

Thought for the day: *There's no choice when it comes to quality.*

The Couple Who Got a Second Chance

*Listen to advice and accept instruction, that you may gain
wisdom for the future.*

—Proverbs 19:20

There was once a certain man who was thumbs up on
marriage but who had difficulty in finding a permanent partner,
three having already sought greater happiness by way of
domestic courts. Then chance did cause him to meet a woman
with a similar track record.

When they saw how much they had in common, they knew
right away that they were naturals for the until-death-do-us-part
ritual. So they got a proper license, two wedding bands inscribed
with initials and interlocking hearts, and went in search of a
clergyman to OK their splendid plan with a memorable
occasion.

Now they found one unpacking his books, having just moved
from another state. When they told him how it was, he asked a
few questions calculated to give him a better view of things.
With his experience he could tell this was no made-in-heaven
arrangement. So he urged them to listen to his advice and accept
instruction that they might gain wisdom for the future. Using
words not to offend, he said he did not see them making it past
the second turn in the primrose path, and the choice of wisdom
for them was separate ways.

They told him their hearts were already pulsating in unison so
please get on with the knot tying. They were impatient to get a
half nelson on happiness.

God's ambassador then rounded up the janitor and church
secretary to witness this sacred moment at the altar. He gave his
best lasting-impression emphasis to key phrases. The couple
then traded rings, were fully pronounced, after which all papers

were properly signed and one sent posthaste to the county clerk. The husband and wife went toward their future and the minister to his books.

Now being new in the state the clergyman did not know that to be a proper Marryin' Sam he had to register at the court house as one duly qualified. This knowledge was officially proclaimed to him the day his signed marriage license reached the county clerk's office. The marriage was null and void, and, yes, the couple would have to get another blood test before a new license could be issued. Sorry, the ways of God and men do have their differences.

The clergyman left his books and went to see the couple, rehearsing as he went several lines designed to take him off the hook. But in each case he came out the fall guy. So he'd just give them a straight-from-the-shoulder version—which he did. There was nothing to do, he told them, but a repeat performance clear from the top.

The erstwhile bridegroom saw no problem and thought they could take care of it right away. Didn't his wife think so, too? Whereupon, she said this was an excellent time to call it quits in her best so-long-it's-been-good-to-know-you.

When the stunned clergyman reached home, his wife asked for a what-happened, and he could only say, "You'll never believe it!"

Thought for the day: *Good solutions do not compound the problem.*

The Little Boy
Who Was Big on Happiness

*Then I shall come to you, in the purpose of God, with a
happy heart, and may even enjoy with you a little holiday.*
                    —Romans 15:32 (Phillips)

Once a certain six-year-old was overcome with generous
feelings and planned an immediate what-to-do-about-it without
benefit of outside consultation. He would be the Easter Bunny
for the grown-ups along his street and bring them joy with the
help of colored eggs his mother would dye for him as soon as she
learned of his timely plan, it being already the day before Easter.

News of his splendid idea did reach her as she Sherlock-
Holmesed a strange sound in the storage closet. It was dress
rehearsal time, and he had on an old white flannel costume
complete with long pink-lined ears and a fluffy cotton tail.

She asked for a how-come, and he gave it to her in excited
generalities. Which, when interpreted, meant that he'd miracu-
lously stumbled onto a path of civilized behavior. She gave the
well-known what's-a-mother-to-do sigh, and his day proceeded
according to master plan.

Except he nearly blew it a couple of times, his strong suit
being uncontrolled enthusiasm. He gave off with constant
why-don't-you advice liberally mixed with hurry-up chatter.
And did she think he should hop from house to house on all
fours, or walk standing up like usual? A quick trial run around
the kitchen floor gave him a ready answer.

Then performance time. The colored eggs were nestled gently
in a basket properly chosen for such a high and personal
occasion and lined with soft artificial grass. He was costumed in
marshmallow white; the long ears flopped just right to get votes
for the isn't-he-darling award.

Mother thought there should be mascara whiskers to make him look like a real bunny. But this was thumbs down. He wanted it known this bunny was he. His neighborhood deportment had been on the skids. If any gold stars were handed out for doing generous things, he wanted them on the right card.

Before he left, Mother asked for a command performance, which she got. He stood tall and said he was coming to the door with a happy heart to enjoy a little holiday with the people, and if they'd take an egg from his basket they'd have a happy heart, too.

He bunny-hopped out the door and at every house there was a standing ovation which made his happiness grow more with each new stop.

Then he bounded right up to a strange house where a lady simply opened the door and said, "I don't want to buy any" and closed it right then and there.

Thought for the day: *A misunderstanding is hard to correct.*

The Boy Who Thought He Had It Coming

It is more blessed to give than to receive.
—Acts 20:35c

There was once a certain boy who had been deprived of deprivation. While he was yet three he had had his fair share of the good life as approved by the Association of Toy Manufacturers. And thanks to TV commercials on children's shows he could see that there was even more to behold and enjoy:

"Mommy, can I have that?"

"Daddy, I want this."

"Can I have it, can I?"

Early in the game the parents did a this-we-agree, and it was to be nix on the plastic temporaries designed to qualify as solid waste. Instead it would be a few items of selected quality and substance which would be a joy forever to their son.

Now there lived in that same country aunts, uncles, grandparents, and special friends who had not been privy to this noble thought. Each of them being excellent practitioners in the more-blessed-to-give approach and feeling called up to include the certain boy in the practicing of their faith. Being people of low estate, each knew it was not the gift but the thought that really counted. So in no time at all his room was full of parental frustration.

The young consumer had learned the art of persuasion and could route almost any shopping trip through a toy department and end with a satisfied smile.

Then one day there came a cease-and-desist order by way of the head of the household. It was forcefully issued with a spontaneous soliloquy with the enough-junk-for-a-lifetime theme. It carried the marvelous moral that character was built in learning that one did not get things just because they were there. Having thus proclaimed and being much impressed with the persuasive powers of his voice, he left it to his wife to develop the necessary operational procedure, and she did.

The next day was shopping, but not as usual. The certain boy heard the orders of the day: The travels through the marketplace would not include the toy department. It was to be understood that he did not get things each time they went out—today being one of those times. These orders included selected direct quotes from his father.

Now this impressed him not at all. Once safely in the department store he did his best I-want-a-toy routine. But this only got him the what-did-I-tell-you. So he did same song, second verse. But this time it was on the dead run toward you know where.

The long arm of parental authority gave him a not-so-fast. It clamped hard to his wrist, which caused his knees to go limp, his eyes to leak, all the while exclaiming in loud, persecuted tones of his heartfelt desires.

There in front of God and everybody the mother of her son swallowed her pride which gave her a red face, determined that school was still in session. He would learn the lesson. It was exit left through the revolving door with him dragging feet all the way.

He kept the sound effects going all the way home. Then he jumped from the car and ran into the house. There he found grandmother with her arms out, saying, "Don't cry. Look what I brought you."

He opened the sack. It was a new red fire truck.

Thought for the day: *Life teaches strange lessons.*

31

The Influential Ecclesiastic
Who Gave His Support

And the king [David] vowed, ". . . Solomon shall be the
next king and sit upon my throne."
                                    —I Kings 1:29-30b (TLB)

There was once an old faithful of the ecclesiastical crowd who
went to the church's annual convention ready for business. That
business was finding a replacement for the denomination's top
position, the current occupant was heading for pasture due to
age.

Anytime Old Faithful released a my-thoughts-on-the-matter
bulletin everyone listened twice. After all, he held down a blue
ribbon church which showed he knew a thing or two. Not to
mention those royalty checks from his books which were
considerable. Then too he had the art of persuasion down to an
inspiring voice complete with selected facts.

All delegates agreed that the top position should go to the
right person. Just who that was God only knew—and he'd
speak his mind through majority vote, being in favor of
democracy as he was. However, Old Faithful was a reliable
advance man. So one should lean his way to keep check on the
windage.

The top job was no snap. Instead it was known as a "real
challenge." So to make it somewhat bearable the office holder
also received prestige, power, an attractive salary, with a
matching house and expense account, plus other considerations.

There was one among them who found these conditions of life
to be the very ones that brought out the best in him. Naturally he
felt morally obligated to do his best. So he backroomed Old
Faithful with a help-me. He got the thumbs up.

Right away the influential man and his crew worked the hallways, lobbies, and coffee breaks, maneuvering their bandwagon to head the parade. In no time their man was a no-doubt-about-it lead-pipe cinch. It was plain to see that the secret ballot was now a formality. With it in the bag like it was the inner circle had a victory celebration.

Now there was a contrary notion at this convention. And a holder of it buttonholed the man of pasturing age. The contrary notion gave him a complete do-you-know-what's-happening report. Whereupon the old top man threw in with the Other Guy. This sent hey-did-you-hear waves all through the convention. It was so unsettling that the final vote gave the Other Guy the marbles. Whereupon Old Faithful packed his bags and retired to his blue ribbon church in a hurry.

Now the Other Guy had not been out to lunch during Old Faithful's lobbying. He thought and thought about it. With the mantle of leadership wrapped around him his way became clear. If Old Faithful made such a dreadful mistake when the right direction was obvious, how capable was he in the uncertain matters? The kingdom would be better served if he were transferred to an out-of-the-way place where such weaknesses could do no harm—which is what happened.

Thought for the day: *Backing a loser has a limiting future.*

The Woman
Who Set Her Mind for Tomorrow

Do not boast about tomorrow, for you do not know what a day may bring forth.

—Proverbs 27:1

There once was a woman who'd had it up to here with household clutter. She proclaimed tomorrow round-up time; destination—the city dump. As trail boss she'd already eyed most of the critters that were to go. With the main herd out of the way, swinging back for stragglers would be a cinch.

Now her long-time partner noticed that most of the first-to-go category fell under the heading "Personal Possessions—His." He did a holy bovine demanding a how-come. So in a tone that was for sure she said it was mostly his stuff that made their home look like a collection drop for a rummage sale.

She showed him pictures in her favorite life-can-be-beautiful magazine, the kind that featured homes of the neat and orderly variety. This is the way, she said, home should look, there being no place for the miscellaneous items he and the children attracted like magnets.

Well, he told her she should not be taken in by fictitious photography. Not one picture showed dirty socks on the floor. Then, too, having a tidy house and garage at the same time was strictly no way. Besides it was contrary to the American way of life.

Such oratory did not dissuade her vote for neatness. She just pulled out a drawer that was a depository for everything from plastic can tops and postage stamps to a broken pocketknife. She did this with a tell-me-about-it expression. "It's my treasure drawer," he said.

But why, she wanted to know, did every drawer have to be a treasure drawer and totally disorganized. He said, "To confound burglars."

He saw that she persisted. So he agreed to help create this way of life of which she boasted. However, they would ride the range together and do selective cutting instead of engaging in a wholesale drive. She agreed, and they'd start tomorrow, it being Saturday.

They began their work in the garage judging critters from different points of view. Hers was for immediacy, his the long-range consideration. Like the hamster cage with the homemade look of quality: It should go because Betsy, now ten, said she no longer wanted such animals. But the long-time partner pointed out that seven-year-old Buddy might become a houser of nature. So the cage became a wait-and-see item. And likewise for the aquarium.

They proceeded without progress for some time, then adjourned to the house. They were just agreeing to dispose of a five-year supply of *Backyard Nature* magazines when: Enter two children. Mood: Excitement and enthusiasm! They carried a crushed metal bucket, a worn-out music box, and a keen poster.

People on the next street had just moved, leaving behind a pile of neat junk. The other kids hadn't found it yet. Before the range riders could say anything, their children were running up the street pulling their wagon behind them.

Thought for the day: *There's staying power in a way of life.*

The Day the Wife
Was Taken for a Ride

*The fountains of the great deep burst forth, and the
windows of the heavens were opened.*
—*Genesis 7:11*b

One day a member of the good-and-stable variety was going
nowhere in particular when his route led him past Crow's
Sporting Goods Store. He braked his pace ever so slightly to
notice an inflated raft in the window. Just then inspiration put
the bear hug on his thoughts and would not turn loose. So he
went inside and bought a raft.

Then he hurried home to tell his wife he was going rafting
down a river. She was eligible to come under the family plan.
Together they would have a happy time like those people
pictured in Crow's store window.

She did the dumfounded, then regained composure and made
judgments about his mentality. She demanded a previous-
experience accounting for such an outing. Trips through the
amusement park's Old Mill did not count.

He was way ahead of her, having already read the illustrated
pamphlet included in the price of purchase. It would all be a
nothing-to-it. She could take his word for that. Once in the
current it was lean-back time in which to compose memorable
experiences.

Having heard about white water, she asked where he was
going to find this flow-gently-sweet-Afton. The inspired man
was not a born-yesterday. He'd picked the brains of the man at
Crow's. He worked only on Saturdays and got his kicks from
trail-biking rough country, but had rafting friends. He pinpointed
their favorite spot which was a six- to eight-hour float.

All this the inspired man explained with a trust-me look

complete with a description of how the raft rode over rough water like clouds on air currents. As he talked he came to believe himself and was soon standing straight and trustworthy in his own eyes. She agreed to go.

The next Saturday they pushed into a slow current, having arranged for a downstream pick-up. His enthusiasm brightened the cloudy sky, and he laughed at the goodly breeze saying now they would travel faster. In a short time she put on her glad-I-came look, and they both leaned back, gathering memorable experiences.

Two hours later, rounding a bend, they thought they heard a diesel truck driving up the river. Suddenly the fountains of the deep burst forth, turning the river into a roller coaster. The raft bent forward, backward, and sideways at the same time. The windows of heaven opened and rain plummeted to earth. The wind blew harder.

The current used the raft as a battering ram trying to dislodge large boulders, all with a discouraging effect upon the occupants' morale. This uncommon sight captured the inspired man's attention and held his eyes at the wide-open position.

His wife screamed for him to do something. Since this situation had not been covered in the illustrated pamphlet, he did what he thought best. He held on, and did it with some conviction.

The river and rain persisted in this condition for some time. It seemed like forty days but it wasn't really. Only about four hours. Then the fountains of the deep and the windows of heaven were closed. The couple drifted into a calm stretch which marked the trip's end.

As they pushed to the low bank to beach the raft he said, "See, I told you I knew how to do it!"

Thought for the day: *If it weren't for trust, one would never go anyplace.*

The Store Manager
Who Showed His Stuff

Those who think themselves great shall be disappointed and humbled.

—Matthew 23:12 a (TLB)

Claude managed a retail department store for a nationwide firm. He decorated his office with photographs of himself standing beside important people. Some had friendly words written across the bottom. Also in plain view were plaques suitably inscribed to let the world know he was making it big in the business jungle. Claude plain-sighted these so people could tell at a glance that he was a valuable piece of merchandise. This eliminated the need to pat himself on the back and risk injuring his elbow.

Being a gilt edge it was a sure thing that he owned a large likeness of the company president. It showed the president with his arm around Claude's shoulder, both smiling friendly like. This hung right over Claude's black executive chair. He would sit there and strike a pose of authority when conferring with underlings.

He'd let the hired help know that he was in this store instead of others because he did not want a snap position. Challenge was the only thing in life that counted. He was shrewd in the clutches, driving bargains into the ropes.

His specialty was turning losing propositions into blue chips. So things were to be done his way or the help knew where to pick up their pay. When talking like this the valuable piece paused now and again to spit out chunks of tenpenny nails so listeners would know it was not idle chatter.

One day a couple of the higher echelon variety from the home office came for an unannounced how's-it-going visit. That meant they wanted a look-see at the books to count the number of digits left of the decimal, and also to be sure they were written in the proper color of ink.

When they finished they had some exciting advice for Claude. He was so happy for any suggestion that he simply bent over backwards to listen. He went back so far that he ended on the floor. Then he brushed himself off so the higher echelons would not get their shoes dusty while walking on him.

They walked so hard that they'd stamped the breath right out of the valuable piece. He was not in condition for this kind of treatment. So the help knew the jungle fighter had been outstalked when he left for home.

As soon as he saw his wife he started the what-a-day opening. But she cut him off with her leave-your-business-at-the-office rule. Besides she was in a hurry. She and some friends were giving that new beach resort a two-day try. So he'd have to walk the poodle since she had not had time. Then Mother wanted some books, and he was to get them to her by 7:30. There might be something in the refrigerator to eat but she wasn't sure. And, oh yes, she'd cashed a check for a bundle. In doing so she got her stubs mixed up and might be overdrawn. He could look into it if he thought it important.

With that she was gone. The valuable piece did the assignments. Then he went back to the office and sat alone in his big chair. He looked at all his pictures and awards, remembering how important he was.

Thought for the day: *Some people are more easily impressed than others.*

The Helpful Husband
Who Attracted Attention

It is better to suffer for well-doing . . . than for doing wrong.

—*I Peter 3:17 (NEB)*

Oscar was a husband top-rated in combining a helpful heart with more-trouble-than-you're-worth abilities. Since they'd worn the shine off their marriage and were now down to the bare wood, Elsie had ceased trying to change him. Outmaneuvering was the primary objective.

Still she had collected a storehouse of you-wouldn't-believes. These were items stuffed with exceptional conversational value which she served up at her weekly bridge table. Real head-shakers that had the listeners remembering others of Oscar's kind.

Who but an Oscar would put away dishes from the dishwasher before they'd been washed. (Elsie admitted she was a careful rinser.) And in helping with the groceries no one did a better open-the-egg-carton-upside-down act than Oscar. The results cleaned up fast with him and the dog working together. It went even faster if it had been freshly waxed. Once to make amends for his zealousness he went to repair the leaky faucet without turning off the water pressure. It all happened with Elsie trying to cook dinner.

Now she did not wish to cold-water his helpful heart, but she had suffered from his well-doing long enough. So she devised certain field maneuvers calculated to keep him out of the house. She employed these with dispatch when getting ready for special occasions—like Saturday when there were those dropping in by special invitation for a full sit-down dinner.

On that appointed day she told Oscar all was well except for a few items: fancy paper napkins and four twelve-inch blue tapers for the table. Like a dear, he could pick them up at the department store. The helpful heart leaped at the opportunity. He arrived there to find himself in the midst of a sale in which all participants agree to suspend rules governing polite society. These to be reactivated only after all present have satisfied their avarice or when the merchandise disappears—whichever comes first.

He did the side-shoulder wedge trying to make it to the candle counter in one piece. Just then the helpful heart noticed a young mother. She was trying to make it out the door loaded down with parcels and two children in tow. Right away he did the boy scout bit, desiring to take her packages in a helpful way.

She was misconstruing his offer for well-doing. As they tugged ever so briefly two men who did not support law and order passed them as though they were late for an appointment. One relieved the mother of her purse, and the other knocked the helpful heart to the floor.

Before Oscar could sound an alarm a house security guard did a johnny-on-the-spot and accused Oscar of setting up the vanishing act. His wallet had disappeared along with the mother's purse so he could not identify himself properly. This earned him a trip to the police station with several charges pending. At which time he was told he could make one phone call.

He did. Elsie answered and interrupted his "Hello, dear" by saying cookies were in the oven, and he'd have to call later. She hung up, leaving the helpful heart looking right into the hard eyes of the desk sergeant and wondering why it was the righteous who suffered.

Thought for the day: *Being helpful is a special art.*

The Company That Paid
for Some Good Advice

Some of your number are loafing, busybodies instead of busy.

—*II Thessalonians 3:11 (Moffatt)*

In the manufacturing world was a certain toy and novelty company holding its own in a discouraging sort of way. Doing well was a novelty not included in its usual line. But it was willing to make it a regular, demand being what it was.

To get going on a good return without fumbling the ball in the end zone, the officers called a specialty team in from the sidelines. This team knew all about business management and divining preventatives against waste and inefficiency. Any company following their good advice would save several times the cost of their splendid recommendations which came bound in a three-color cover. Obviously, then, they should be considered assets rather than liabilities.

So this team of assets came into the game with forms, questionnaires, and queries high on the recommended list by the professor at the university who taught Business Survey No. 424. These were especially devised to provide essential data for a picture of the company's overall operation. Routine stuff and nothing for the workers to get upset over.

Being trained assets as they were, they knew every business had loafers and busybodies. Flushing them was priority one. This was a snap with their properly interpreted data. It gave them the scent, leading them straight to the research and development department.

Would you believe that there, twelve employees did nothing but sit around and think, carrying on idle conversation! The properly evaluated data showed that sit-around thinking carried the lowest of all efficiency ratings. Three or four persons putting their whole minds to it could do the necessary brain work. The rest could apply for early retirement.

With these savings the company could add several accountant types to the payroll as reinforcements for the business manager. He was going to need help in quarterbacking the strategy detailed in the final report with the three-color cover. It was pure orchids that he'd been able to do the job thus far shorthanded as he was.

Now all of this did come to pass. The newly acquired read fiscal literature and looked around to start practical application to show they were earning their keep. In no time at all they came up with a unanimous: Subcontract the packaging operation.

Imagine their surprise to discover this newly emptied space was just right to house the computer processing equipment. A necessary addition to keep on top of waste and inefficiency.

Of course, it was obvious that the additional personnel coming would need desk space. They were agreeable to working cramped until the sales department gave up their offices. After all, the charts and diagrams showed that since the sales force was on the road most of the time they had little need of permanent office space. There were corners here and there big enough for a chair and table.

Each month more people signed on to keep waste and inefficiency under control. It became such a monumental operation that a new wing had to be built so they had space to sit in.

In a few years the company divested itself of the manufacturing of toys and novelties. It became a consultant firm specializing in business management—because that was what they knew best.

Thought for the day: *Advice carries its own consequences.*

The Ministers
Who Found the Way in a Storm

Seek, and you will find; knock, and it will be opened to you.

—*Matthew 7:7*b

In a blessed section of the city the spirit of cooperation dwelled among six ministers, each of a different persuasion. They knew that the Kingdom was thumbs down on any church trying to go it alone. So their burning desire was to show that they were in step and doing it by the numbers.

How this was to be done was their great yet-to-be-discovered. But to make sure they all pulled on the same oar they agreed on a monthly luncheon approach. It was the $2.25 special, complete with a private room, snappy retorts from the waitress, and vanilla custard.

But before putting their flocks on open range each wanted to be sure none of his sheep would be tempted to stray into another fold. So the first of these exciting meetings was the sizing-up-the-other-guy variety.

It began with a much-obliged to God, then an exchange of the latest in ecclesiastical humor, and finally the discovery that in the eyes of God there was not a favorite among them. Each was managing a low-budget production because of box-office decline. They had naught to fear from each other and with this knowledge the spirit of oneness prevailed.

Then a self-appointed chairman took over the meeting. With the help of *Robert's Rules of Order*—a free translation—the six quickly agreed on the manner in which they would display their united strength and strike a blow for the Kingdom: "Let us choose a problem of magnitude which is bringing grievous concern to the people. Surround it, sound the trumpet, gang tackle it, and make it cry 'Uncle!' "

With hallelujahs they adjourned into the world, each searching for a Jericho, their findings to be reported at the next meeting. And that is what happened.

As ice water and coffee flowed, they discussed in brilliant and remarkable fashion every isn't-it-awful that had come to their attention. But for all their splendid abilities they could not find a way of advancing their united forces over the terrain close enough to the problem to blow the trumpet.

But the small army of the Lord was not dismayed. They were filled with the conviction that they need only seek and they would find, knock, and it would open.

They continued the meeting into the next month . . . and the next . . . and the next with the self assurance that in this great world of problems there was something they could do together.

Then one night late in the week black clouds darkened the heavens, cold air moved in from the north, and snow began to fall. Now snow in this city was a twice-in-a-decade happening. And on this occasion it did not stop until it lay three feet on the level.

The next morning one of the would-be Joshuas, whose bedroom window commanded a good view of the church parking lot, looked from his pillow and saw what the night had wrought. He lay meditating on this unusual sight when suddenly he beheld a vision and glory shown 'round about him. He called his fellow clergymen and told them of his great sight. They all agreed that what he had seen should come to pass.

And so the six did hire the same man to clear the snow from their church parking lots.

Thought for the day: *The dedicated do not remain idle.*

The Woman Who Was Ready
for a New Year's Party

Oil and perfume bring joy to the heart, but cares torment a man's very soul.

—Proverbs 27:9 (NEB)

Once there was a young woman named Tillie Schwartz who was of the lonely type with evenings to match. Her social calendar was filled with blanks. She'd tried several what-to-do-about-its in the form of beauty concoctions heralded by houses of cosmetics. However, the special ingredients must have been left out of her jars. It was very depressing.

Approaching New Year's Eve made Tillie think about galas and frivolities. They were qualities of life she sought. To find them in the accompaniment of others would be thrilling. Should the other be in the form of a man, ecstasy itself. Of course, not just any man. She had standards. The first being he'd have to ask her out. With that principle fulfilled she'd give consideration to the others in due course.

Now there was a shining ray of hope for Tillie this year. He worked in the stock room and came topside according to a stated schedule. He had difficulty initiating conversation. He also carried a retiring personality. So retiring that some suspected him to be dead. Except that he swayed from one foot to the other whenever he stood in one place.

Lately the shining ray was lunching with Tillie, both being brown baggers. On occasions he was so bold as to buy her coffee from the vending machine. With her woman's intuition she knew from this that he was just twisted up inside to ask her out for New Year's. But since he could not form the words and time was growing short, Tillie decided to help him meet her initial standard.

On the fateful day she came to work wearing her best looker and just enough $35 perfume to do the trick. As the saleslady said, the perfume gives a girl confidence and brings joy to the heart. From the way he smiled at her during lunch she knew the perfume was hard at it. So she eased into her premeditated subject. There were going to be lots of house parties, she said. And she proceeded to describe them in exhilarating detail.

The shining light was so caught up in her words that he almost said something. But before he could swallow his bite of tuna salad he remembered he did not have any invitation to a house party. He remained silent and took another bite.

Tillie shifted the subject ever so slightly. Many, she said, go out to fine supper clubs for the celebration. Paper hats, horns, confetti, live dance music, oh, it's fun. The shining ray knew this, of course. He also knew that his accumulated wealth would not reach past the salad. He kept on chewing.

At last Tillie became desperate. She discarded principle number one and came right out and said that she'd fix a steak dinner at her house for the two of them. How nice it would be to dine together, toasting in the New Year alone.

He jumped to his feet and swayed violently from side to side. Alone with a woman for several hours! Whatever would he talk about for so long? His soul was tormented with the vision of it all. Then he blurted right out loud, "I spend New Year's Eve with Mother!" and disappeared into the stock room leaving Tillie with one more blank.

Thought for the day: *Abandoning principles seldom pays off.*

The Couple Who Got the Jump on Christmas

Every mountain and hill shall be made low . . . and the rough places plain.

—Isaiah 40:4 (KJV)

It was the this-year-will-be-different season again. And in a certain household all agreed that Christmas should be enjoyed, not dreaded.

The man of this house did say, "This year let us clear the hurdles early by doing a fast start. I'm tired of pounding down to the wire in a dead heat. This will give us a chance to get into the grandstand and watch Christmas come down the stretch."

His wife gave him a count-me-in-and-show-me-how reply. Which he did.

He turned the dining room table into a make-room-for-action. In the center he put all things needful, accompanied by some illuminating instructions.

One end of the table, he said, was for wrapping gifts as soon as they might be brought into the house. Any gift could be wrapped in twenty minutes. Then it would be finished instead of stacked in the closet waiting for its time to come. The other end was for Christmas cards. These to be addressed and signed in those odd ten-and fifteen-minute periods that clutter up the day.

Immediately he sat down and knocked off ten cards and three letters, finishing with a "See what I mean."

His wife said it would be crowded eating around the breakfast bar, but what was four or five days of inconvenience compared to the blessings that would be theirs when the mountains surrounding Christmas had been brought low and the rough places made smooth.

By Friday they had excavated two mountains, which called for a TV break. The break lasted for three weekend football games, plus the Monday night special. Priority was given to the gift list during commercials and half times.

The wife did take the list into the marketplace. There she found several excellent suggestions with prices to match. That sent her back home for further consultation and created a temporary work stoppage on the mountain project.

But this could be handled, especially if they finished the rest of the cards that evening. However, he did a not-available, there being a twenty-five-dollar cash prize at the office for the best Christmas decoration, and he was just made committee chairman for his department. That, however, should not keep her from digging in.

She announced she was eliminated from the home show for at least two days due to a conflict of interest. Tonight began the PTA bazaar preliminaries, with the gala affair on Friday. And as long as they were talking, when was he going to get up their outdoor lights.

Not until after the weekend, he told her, because that's when he opened at Sixth and Center as a bell ringer in the put-something-in-the-pot production.

One day followed another. The family continued crowding around the breakfast bar for meals with the dining room table piled high with all things needful.

Thought for the day: *Early planning often shows.*

The Minister
Who Asked and Received

Now it happened that as he was praying alone the disciples were with him; and he asked them, "Who do the people say that I am?"

—Luke 9:18

Once there was a minister whose Friday habit was a face with the expression drained out and his eyes fixed beyond the here and now.

While people debated whether this was piety or conceit, he wondered whether to ask the Lord to halt the sun or to simply go back to selling mail-order shoes—it now being the fifth day and his sermon was yet far from him.

Since Monday he'd tried to slow waltz a sermon idea, but before he could get a firm grip on it the music would stop.

And for the following reasons: a report to the finance committee, a phone query about the interpretation of a scripture verse, an invocation for the Annual Meeting of The Citizens for Humanity, a newspaper announcement, the weekly bulletin, a presurgical call on a parishioner with an ingrown nail, a specially called how-to-keep-morale-high-while-discouraged meeting for church school teachers, a luncheon address, and a knock on the door from a salt-of-the-earth who was passing out God's blessings for the price of a meal.

The fabric he had managed to weave from his inspiring thoughts as he traveled through this obstacle course resembled that of the Emperor's New Clothes. He decided to take his temperature to see if he might be catching the flu. He was not, so his mind went back to selling shoes.

Each week was the same—quarterbacking the final minutes against the clock. While he always came through with a three-pointer right between the anthem and the benediction, the strain had him shouting, "Who am I, anyway? A preacher or an office boy; a theologian or a fund raiser; a physician of the soul or a Sunday school recruitment officer?"

Before he could answer himself it was time again to play beat-the-clock. And he went about the house penalizing his family for delay of game.

One day he came to himself and said, "I am tired of being on my eight-yard line. I will get a better field position if I explain my dilemma to the people. I will ask them to help me decide which of my many duties gets top billing and how much time I should give to each of them. Then I can organize my work and give proper time and thought to all things."

He sent his flock a let-us-reason-together letter enclosing a proper questionnaire for their consideration and for his edification.

The ecclesiastical pollster then purchased a large columnar pad, sharpened his pencils, and faithfully compiled the results, which he announced the following Sunday.

Of his eleven separate duties, seven finished first in a dead heat with the rest running a close second. All of which, the people said, he could easily handle in eighty-seven hours a week.

Thought for the day: *Almost everyone has an opinion.*

The Reporter Who Did His Thing

You will know the truth, and the truth will make you free.
— John 8:32

There was once a certain reporter working his way through life. He wore a whisk broom mustache, a tweed sport coat with frayed sleeves, baggy pants, and shoes shined last week. He also had a pocket-sized notebook, a pencil, a desk typewriter, and a speech on freedom of the press.

His speech was a well-rehearsed gem suitable for both the platform and private gatherings. He was always ready to oblige, whether asked or not—which was quite understandable when one considered what a bastion of democracy the press was.

"One should know the truth and it will make you free," he said. And he documented such penetrating insight with excellent for-instances of power hungry men willing to wool the public's eyes.

He told whoever would listen that the nation's reporters were alert to this ever-lurking danger. These faithful followers of the goddess Truth had sworn to report the truth as long as it could be done by press time. "After all," he said, "if you can't trust a reporter, who can you trust?"

This champion of the press was not just a preacher of the word, he was a doer, also. And he had learned his way around town in order to get the inside stuff. He called the business men by their first names, had stories for the mayor's secretary, and kept a good ear out for sirens.

Now his notebook was his everything. He filled it with selected sayings of important people, and penetrating observations of signs of the times. All of which he recorded in a self-taught shorthand system. This he accurately transcribed if he was able to make out what he'd written.

He could do marvelous things with the contents of his notebook when using the Who, What, Why, When, and Where approach. It was a cinch to reduce a two-hour city council meeting into 300 words, put a research scientist's life work into a lead paragraph, and he could polish a politician's press conference into something the politician could hardly believe.

One day this seeker of truth went to cover a lecturer coming from out of town. The speaker fell into the great-and-privileged category. He was of the philosopher variety who moved in the same circles as Socrates and Plato. He used words as if he had written the dictionary and could talk about life without once mentioning taxes and higher prices. His talk sparked with such wit and humor that the people gave him the standing ovation routine.

The reporter did his notebook bit after which he cornered the lecturer for fifteen minutes, asking him the kind of questions designed to sell newspapers.

Then he hurried back to the office to do the copy, which rated a page five. It was placed just above the ad for Bill's Shoe Store and next to one for Owen's Hardware.

When it was read the next morning there were several important words missing; the quotation marks were in the wrong places; the lecturer was identified with the wrong college; and his name was misspelled.

Thought for the day: *When looking for facts, try the want ads.*

The Churches
That Found Their Strength in Numbers

*Then I saw a new heaven and a new earth. . . . I saw the
holy city, new Jerusalem, coming down out of heaven from
God.*

*—Revelation 21:1-2*a

The first of each month was sackcloth and ashes for a certain
church treasurer. He had all things needful for his work except
financial backing—check blanks, past-due bills, and fingernails
especially chewed for the occasion.

Among the membership were many who believed the church
would run on what the other guy gave. They knew the story of
the fishes and loaves and admonished the treasurer to "go and
do likewise." He admitted, however, that his praying did not
turn his five clams into surplus and he still eeny, meeny, miney,
moed the bills.

In his annual report he recommended that all months have five
Sundays. To which the church school superintendent took
exception. "We can't get teachers to last out the year now," she
said. "The field is white to the harvest, but my Timothys and
Tituses are extinct, and the Dorcases are in short supply." She
proposed a three-Sunday month.

A compromise motion was immediately proposed, seconded,
and passed that the number of Sundays remain as they were and
to seek other solutions to the problems.

Now there were in the same neighborhood yet two other
churches with like afflictions, each being composed of the
faithful few with bowed backs and blisters from rowing short
handed against a strong current. Then one of their kind, pausing
to take a deep breath, took view of their backward progress. He
also caught sight of the other two boats trying the impossible.

Right then he did a soapbox about being fed up with this going-down-with-the-ship syndrome, and why not all get into the same boat and testify to the faith with a full crew and powerful strokes.

As he spoke, the suffering servants felt the aches in their backs and the pains in their hands. It was "Hear! Hear!"

Then committee time. Its task was to lay the course to the land of dreams come true. In due time they neared the Promised Land and the glory of God did shine 'round about them, properly witnessed by the local press.

On the first Sunday inside the church the new age dawned: teacher in every classroom, a full choir complete with director and organist, pews tightly packed, and grateful expressions did overflow in the offering plates. The minister preached of the remnant of Israel and told of what strengths from God lie with the few who keep the faith.

The members of the remnant nodded in agreement, for the truth of these words was now plain to them. They looked around and saw their great numbers and were satisfied that their struggles had not been in vain.

In their new-found strength they caught sight of a new heaven and a new earth and saw the new Jerusalem coming down around them. Then one by one they leaned contentedly upon their oars and they remembered pain no more.

It came to pass that once again the treasurer chewed his nails, and the church school superintendent dreamed of three-Sunday months.

Thought for the day: *It takes more to improve the herd than just putting them in the same pasture.*

The Young Man
Who Was Disposed to Become Famous

There is a way which seems right to a man, but its end is the way to death.

—*Proverbs 16:25*

Little Stanley Arbuckle had a way about him that attracted attention. He walked around in a skinny frame, looked at the world through thick glasses, and cried a lot. This made him perfect for teasing—a fact known to his schoolmates. Just to spite them, Stanley decided to grow up and become famous.

How he was to accomplish this remarkable feat was not clear. Which was why Stanley went to college so as to decide on a suitable star to harness. But once there he was amazed at how much there was that did not interest him. This clouded the direction of his future. So Stanley adjusted his glasses with his left hand and settled down as a so-so student choosing not to hurry destiny.

In boring classes the thought of what the profs might say in days ahead when they realized that such a famous one as he had sat in their classes almost made Stanley chuckle out loud. And the success story that would be in the alumni magazine! What would his classmates say? "Stanley Arbuckle? Why, I went to school with him. What do you know!"

After college it came to him that he should be doing something while awaiting the beams of fame's klieg lights. So he talked to a book company about a place under the sun. They gave him a sample case, a canned speech, and he walked away an encyclopedia salesman.

Of course, Stanley knew all along this was only a sideline. But being associated with great ideas like he now was gave him an inspiration. He should write. He had nothing to say, but the practice of literary skills would put him ahead of the game when that best-selling idea came along. So he bought a how-to book and inflicted himself on the two-cents-a-word market. And one day he made it in the *Hardware Journal* with a dandy 1,000-worder informing retail clerks the best way to smile at customers.

This sale plus his encyclopedia commission was very little, which forced a change in Stanley's work. He dropped from sight by way of signing on as a case worker with a governmental agency dealing in human miseries as defined by statute. He surfaced now and then as an actor in a local amateur theatre. Then he'd sink back into the statute routine.

Stanley was going down for the third time when he grabbed hold of an offer as head man in the local chapter of Youth Organization, Inc. It carried a good salary to anyone who could raise the budget. The pressure of accomplishing this shoved his real-life ambitions out of mind.

But one day they all flooded back when he was arranging the hospitality bit for a certain celebrity coming to town for a good cause. Stanley gave it his best, which included following the important person wherever he went. This was an eye-opener. Stanley watched the celebrity shake hands with everyone, wear a frozen smile, try to give each person his undivided attention, and respond to inane comments as though they were real gems.

Stanley knew that a life like this would be the death of him. He was very pleased that he hadn't gotten around to becoming a famous person.

Thought for the day: *We don't always know what is good for us.*

The Shepherd Who Had It Spelled Out

Moses returned home and talked it over with Jethro, his father-in-law.

—Exodus 4:18a (TLB)

In the days when there were many gods to choose from, a man named Moses leaned against the shady side of a rock. Thoughtfully he stroked his beard trying to digest what had happened. The day started pleasantly enough as he brought his father-in-law's sheep here to Mt. Horeb. Then all at once there's this Lord God telling him he's going to Egypt. No ifs, ands, or buts about it! "And don't worry," says the Lord, "I'll be with you."

"Whatever that meant," thought Moses. He'd never met the Lord God before so he could only go on his first impressions. These made the proposed foreign travel less than exciting. For one thing the Lord God went in for big productions. That burning bush routine made that clear. And the things he said would happen in Egypt—that was out of sight.

"Why can't these gods do things natural like," he wondered. "Why must everything be big deals: They act like they're trying to impress each other."

Moses was pretty sure that the Lord God's getting the Hebrews out of Egypt would be a real one up for him on the other gods. But Moses still wondered why the gods just couldn't do their godding among themselves instead of getting people involved.

The Lord God being with him would only mean never knowing what would happen next. Everything would be big, mighty, and unexpected. Home looked very peaceful to him right now. He lived tax-free in a nice country home and had a steady job with his father-in-law. How could he beat that? Why choose Egypt?

Thinking made Moses hungry. He opened a sheepskin pouch and slurped down some curds. Then he went back to his thoughts about the Lord God as he wiped the drippings off his beard.

"He seemed so secretive," he said to himself. "Why?"

This bothered Moses. Here's the Lord God ordering him to go to the Hebrews in Egypt and tell them to follow him because God had sent him. Their first question would be, "Which one?"

They knew as well as he did that there were gods here, there, and everywhere. At least one to a mountain and probably many others, too. So what was he to tell them? "Say I AM sent you." Now what kind of name was that!

In disgust he picked up a small stone and threw it down the mountain slope. By the time it rolled to a stop he was remembering the Lord God's temper. Moses' heart beat so hard and fast that he was talking out loud. "All I said was that I wasn't the man for the job when he told me the details. Did he get hot. Why the flame went up three hundred degrees right then. With that God tailing after me there could only be trouble. No talking things over with him. His way and no other." Moses shuddered, thinking of what might happen if someone did cross up the Lord God.

By now the sun hung low in the west and Moses was sure of only one thing. The Lord God wanted the Hebrews out of Egypt and Moses was his chosen leader. He gathered the flock together and returned home to talk it over with Jethro, his father-in-law.

Thought for the day: *Never act without good counsel.*

The Wife Who Had
a Proper Upbringing

A good wife who can find? She is far more precious than jewels.

—Proverbs 31:10

There was once a woman who had a large brood and a head of the household with a weak back. He could lift nothing heavier than a pool cue unless it was Tuesday night. Then he managed a bowling ball by being careful of his position.

His delicate condition required that he stay in bed until the sun was high up except on the days he drew his unemployment check. Then he was a bright-and-early, after which he went to a likely place where he and his cronies discussed the state of things until wee hours.

Now his wife was something else again. As far as she knew, the only way it came was by the sweat of the brow. She quit school at fourteen to nurse mother who was sickly. Father thought it an excellent idea for her to also be cook and housekeeper for him and the boys.

One day while doing her usual fifteen-hour shift, her spouse-to-be passed that way and said she was more precious than jewels to do what she was doing, and why should she waste herself at home when she could have all this with him and marriage too.

And so with benefit of clergy they became one.

As the years passed, she remained true to her upbringing. She looked well to the ways of her household and never ate the bread of idleness. She began each day while it was yet dark. She ironed the clothes, woke the children, fixed their breakfast; and then she did short orders and doubled as an automatic dishwasher in a coffee joint that had not heard of minimum wage laws.

By the end of her shift she had two feet like flat irons, bulging varicose veins, and a long trip home to get supper on by six, hubby having never learned to appreciate late meals.

Next it was fun-and-games chasing the younger set into shut-eye without clubbing. On a good evening she could do it so as not to disturb the weak back snoring on the couch.

With the children down for the count, she turned to a basket of mending contracted by you-know-who from a nearby cleaning establishment. He admitted the pay was poor, yet believed every little bit helped.

Sometimes during the late show she slipped off the harness and kissed the sandman.

Now a certain governmental agency was keeping books on this family. One day a social worker of the female variety made a house call for an inside view of how the wife saw things. The agency woman, because of her splendid education, could tell in a minute that the husband was a no-account. So she asked the harried wife a few questions professionally designed to reveal deep feelings.

She admitted that matrimony was a difficult state, and didn't the social worker find it so. The professional woman confessed that in all her years she had never married.

"Oh, dearie," said the precious jewel, "I feel for you. Ain't single life hell!"

Thought for the day: *If given a chance, one will choose one's own problems.*

The School
That Went In for Harmony

What can I do this day . . . to their children whom they have borne?

*—Genesis 31:43*b

In a certain out-of-the-way place there was a school board with thumbs up for culture. Once at a regularly called meeting it was brought to their attention that the young lacked one important opportunity for proper self-expression: a band of instrumental variety. After a period of high-quality discussion, the board did move, second, and pass a satisfactory remedy. And so there came to this school a band director with proper qualifications. He also drank milk and ate only soft foods.

When he assembled the aspiring virtuosos and heard the sounds they made together, he said, "What can I do this day to these children whom their parents have borne?" He knew it was extra-know-how-after-school-and-on-Saturdays for a slight consideration. It was a marvelous success. For in no time at all they were musicking out of Bennett Band Book No. 2. Sometimes they made it to the double bars in just three tries. In a matter of months they were practicing on a heavy, suitably arranged.

The time had come to show parents what they were getting for their money. So the director set the date for a public spectacle. It was a far-off time, so home folks could clear their calendars, and the band could get numbers into recognizable form.

Practice went on in earnest until the night it gave way to the real thing. The school auditorium filled with parents, assorted relatives, and some neighbors whose TVs were in poor condition. Printed programs were available at the door so there might be no question as to the number being played.

Promptly at 7:30 the band members entered, wearing look-alike gold capes and dark slacks, along with shoes and socks in assorted colors. Each member I-spied the audience, climaxing it with a big smile for the important faces. The director finished his milk and brought up the rear. He gave the audience his best glad-to-see-you, then did the downbeat on a rowser especially selected for a break-away start.

Now it only took a note or two to know that this public spectacle was light on experience. But from the feet tapping everyone could tell the band was determined and knew exactly which bar to play. In fact, only the second trombonist lost his place. But his partner pointed it out to him, getting him back with the pack.

A trumpet player forgot to change keys at the refrain. Here and there were squeaks from the reeds. Once two drummers were on the off beat, but the director went up and down with his arms in a wild sort of way and pounded his right foot heavily on the floor, getting the drummers back on rhythm in time for the whole band to end together.

They stayed with it right to the end of the program, including the audience, which gave a big applause when it finally happened. This earned a standing bow from the band with three players knocking the music off their stands.

After the performance, parents told the children what kind of concert it had been and how glad they were to be there. And a certain wife poured her husband a large glass of milk.

Thought for the day: *Having a family helps.*

The Young Executive
Who Was Taking Care of His Future

For many are called, but few are chosen.
—Matthew 22:14

Horace Dittlemyer trained to become a proper specimen of the public-speaking variety. The elocution gym was a back room at Clancy's Inn. He worked out on Thursday noons with a bunch who taught each other to speak according to the book. It was full of dos and don'ts and other marvelous suggestions on how to expound by the numbers. It made oratory a cinch for the faithful. The bunch practiced on each other and received splendid comments on how to do better next time.

Now Horace did this to get ahead in his job, communications being important as they were. He did junior executive chores with a firm that had office space in seventeen cities, keeping his hand raised volunteering to shoulder the heavy burdens of success. But with so many others doing likewise and so few chosen, he remained in his place. Thus his faithfulness to communication training knew no end.

Horace became a picture of poise and confidence behind a speaker's stand. With his paper resting in front of him he'd stand straight and tall, look at the people deliberately, set his volume control on ''variable,'' then let it come. It came with inflections, modulations, and pauses, while waving his arms so the audience would not lose sight of him.

The bunch entered Horace in their area's annual speech-making contest. He won hands down. This earned him two inches and a suitable likeness in the local press, which an important person saw next morning. He met Horace in the office hallway. The important person offered his congratulations, and called for a command performance with a "By the way, I'm working on a big problem and I would like your thoughts on it."

The star of Horace Dittlemyer was on the rise! He looked around for the podium. Someone forgot to set it up. He stared at his audience of one, dead in the face. Horace gulped, then began with a long pause while his mind went out to round up an introduction. He spotted something, but it was middle-of-the-speech material. Next, he came across an illustration that would be a dandy fit just before the conclusion.

The long pause got longer. He tried waving his arms to let the important person know he was still alive. Someone had tied fifty-pound weights to each wrist and they would not move.

Just as he was considering a coughing fit, an introduction came over the horizon. He herded it into the corral. But before Horace could send it out the chute, one untrained in elocution came by. He spent his spare time with his head under the hood of an antique Willis Knight, explaining the virtues of the car's engine to interested parties. For a change of subject, he sat around a small table holding five cards, studying the expressions on the other players' faces.

The important person invited him to give his ideas on the problem under discussion. The untrained started talking belly to belly, studying the expression of the important person as he did. Whereupon he was invited into a private office for more talk.

As they left, Horace was congratulated once again and told to keep up the good work.

Thought for the day: *Always train for the right event.*

The Idle Farmer
Who Tried It in Politics

*Woe to those who are wise in their own eyes, and shrewd
in their own sight!*

—*Isaiah 5:21*

There was a certain farmer who chewed matchsticks while
waiting for his seed wheat to germinate into a bumper crop. He
lived in town and was a familiar sight on Main Street, it being
five blocks long with SLOW signs posted at either end.

Now this tiller of the soil knew what the government should
be doing and spent his time letting others in on the secret. He
performed this civic duty at the barber shop, the corner café, and
around the snooker table while waiting his turn. His facts came
from TV, but he could not remember which programs, and from
articles he'd read someplace. His logic was not of the textbook
variety.

Devotion to his calling made him a regular at the Black Cat
Café. It was the custom for the business crowd to small talk here
before opening shop. His Mt. Olympus was at the end of the
counter which favored his good ear. Here he oracled thusly:
"Well, I don't know a thing about it, but . . ." Listeners gave
him thumbs up for the accuracy of that remark.

It was agreed by all that one so wise in his own eyes and
shrewd in his own sight should get a proper reward. So they
waited with anticipated delight to trap him in his own logic. But
they reckoned not with his style of mentality. He could stroll
into a trap and without knowing it had been sprung, walk away
with strong faith in his pronouncements, leaving the would-be
victors without spoils.

One day while lining up a shot on the five ball, he expounded on the tax problem. Straightening it out, he said, was as simple as sinking a cushion shot in the side pocket.

After a calculated pause, the other cue holder suggested, "Then instead of just talking, why don't you run for mayor and do something about it?"

The light switch went on in his imagination. There, clear as anything, was a large desk marked "MAYOR," and one well known to him sat behind it. He threw away his match, stashed the cue, and walked in a dignified manner to the newspaper office.

He held a press conference with the editor, announcing his candidacy for mayor. The editor was all joy! And, of course, the new candidate would want weekly advertising space, complete with placards with catchy slogans.

Of course.

The blue-jeaned Jimmy Walker stumped, using the door-to-door method, answering questions on all issues: "Well, I don't know a thing about it, but . . ."

Now the downtown crowd rejoiced greatly. The head was on the chopping block. They counted the days 'til the public execution. Poolroom odds were twenty-to-one favoring the guillotine with no takers.

When the polls closed and ballots were counted, the familiar sight was elected mayor by a five-to-four majority. For two days the only words heard were, "Don't look at me. I didn't vote for him."

Thought for the day: *One does not always know who one's friends are.*

The Team That Rallied Around a Tradition

Faith is the assurance of things hoped for, the conviction of things not seen.

—Hebrews 11:1

Waterfall U's football team had not scored in so long the players thought it was against the rules.

This made the local sports writer do the furrowed brow when composing. One day, however, he spotted a sensational. When archiving through past records, he discovered a school tradition heretofore unrecognized. Every eighth year "The Big Splash" team pulled off the unbelievable against the league's front runner. It had been happening ever since when.

Counting to eight on his fingers, the sports writer knew right off the time for another David and Goliath was here. In the upcoming game Big Splash would square off against a team of human steamrollers. They had buried everything in shoulder pads and were looking for national honors complete with trophy suitably inscribed.

Word of this remarkable tradition reached Big Splash's locker room. One player after another began to wonder. Soon all were looking at each other in wondering ways. Then came a voice from somewhere saying, "Why not!" They gave the coach a what-about-it glance. Right off he thought to win was a splendid idea. It would give him some new lines at the Monday Morning Quarterbacks' Breakfast.

Then someone uncorked the you-gotta-believe bottle; the Faith Genie slipped out and went to work. In no time each player pledged to keep the tradition alive. Being sincere as they were gave them the assurance of their hopes with convictions in a victory not yet seen.

This was all belly-laugh material on the enemy campus. The human steamrollers questioned Big Splash's upstairs condition. Then they called them rude names.

Still, it was true that the Big Splash team moved with sure and certain confidence. When asked about the game the reply was always the same: A slight sneer and "We'll be ready!" And secret practices and razzle-dazzle could only dumbfound the opposition. With all this one just had to believe.

Friday night. Pep rally time in front of the gymn with the important people on the steps. They included old grads who remembered the past upsets in words calculated to inspire and build confidence. The crowd cheered on cue. One by one the team members stood up and said fighting words. All ended in singing the fight song which was a rouser. David was ready for Goliath!

Saturday the team of steamrollers walked on to the gridiron ignorant of the power of the spirit loosed among the home team and fans. They did not sense it on hearing the alma mater sung in inspired fashion. Nor did they know fortune had turned against them when Big Splash won the toss. In their ignorance they just lined up as usual. Then someone planted his right foot into the ball. There was a clash of flesh against flesh with plastic in between. The game was on.

The next day's sports headlines read: "64-Year-Old Tradition Dies in 72-0 Score."

Thought for the day: *Self-confidence gets one started.*

The Preacher Who Was Not
at a Loss for Words

*Let your light so shine before men, that they may see your
good works and give glory to your Father who is in
heaven.*

—*Matthew 5:16*

One day a preacher sat judging himself by the standards of
this world and came out at the bottom of the heap. For him it was
vacationing with a borrowed sleeping bag; a "good" suit with
knees too weary to hold a press; appliances, furniture, and a front
door screen that had a Goodwill look of quality. He knew others
were making it big, but did not know why Lady Fortune dealt
him a losing hand.

Once he did join the affluent society with 10 percent down, 10
percent a month. But he canceled his membership with the help
of a loan on his insurance policy. He sat there dousing himself
with self-despair. Then he remembered that he belonged to the
money-isn't-everything crowd and shook free of the grip of
worldly things.

It came to his remembrance that he was a preacher of stellar
proportions as every Dorcas and Timothy in his congregation
knew. Each Sunday it was a spellbinder. His words were
scriptural and came right from the diaphragm.

Then between 12:03 and 12:12 the people shook his hand and
said splendid things about his message. They told him how life
would be better if only he would mimeograph his inspiring
thoughts so they could meditate upon them.

So he agreed to let his light shine by way of weekly handouts.
And the faithful kept them close at hand in case the TV went on
the fritz.

Just as he was about to sprain his wrists by doing a

two-handed back pat his wife came home. She'd been attending a reception at the home of the leading citizen. His was a well-known story.

He grew up in a family that did not have two to rub together. They survived because there were those who cared—the government having not yet heard of their kind. Before he was of age he set out to make it as best he could, picking up bits and pieces about capital gain, depreciation, tax write-offs, and developing the Midas touch. In time, he put the scissor hold on adversity and was making it faster than his wife could dispose of it. And when it came to knowing how, she was major league. The paintings were originals; the world-travel mementos were authentic; and the furniture was exclusive design.

Besides this, the pauper's son had citations and awards from organizations with long names and autographed portraits from the kind of dignitaries that make copy for *Time* magazine.

The preacher's wife rushed home all aglow. "That is such a beautiful home, and he is really a wonderful person."

"Yes," said her husband, "But he can't preach!"

Thought for the day: *Relativity measures all things.*

The Husband Who Lived by Faith

[He] was strong in faith.
—Romans 4:20b (KJV)

Sidney Sidetrough belonged to the thrifty set. Sarah Applhans practiced total depletion. He stockpiled a little each month into a tidy sum. While a good month for Sarah was balancing out at zero with the help of excellent buys mentioned in the ads. It was only natural that the two should marry, but they contracted together without discussing the by-laws.

Sarah's natural endowments had kept her high on the local most-wanted list. And Sidney had to put forth to outdistance the competition, leaving no time to check out practical matters. This oversight brought Sidney to the end of his bank balance before the third month had past. He called a directors' meeting and announced, "We're living as though there are too many days between paychecks!"

Sarah noticed this too, and what could he do about it? Being cut from kindly cloth, Sidney reasoned that with proper guidance she'd be a dollar-stretcher in no time. She'd lived her early life missing the joys of first-hand fiscal responsibility. So there began the household budget system with proper instructions from himself. She took to it immediately and had a wonderful month with the help of several charge accounts.

The next board meeting was red ink and black crêpe. He proposed that charge accounts receive a final burial. Her allowance would be in cash while he earmarked a goodly amount for the tidy sum. Sarah voted affirmatively.

The month began with confidence and hope. But in two weeks Sidney was going to bed hungry. He asked for a how-come and got the blue-eyed lament: "I've been living on my allowance like you asked. But I can't get what I need and groceries, too."

His remarks were deleted from the minutes. He signed his new stockpile over to the grocer. Yet he was strong in faith! He knew even yet she would become a wizard of domestic finance. He reasoned with her, "You need to worry about your future. I'll turn all financial responsibilities over to you, taking only an allowance for my personal needs. Whether the insurance is paid will be your concern. Why should my sleep be troubled because I may die uncovered. Facing realities you will learn proper budgeting."

She voted "aye."

In no time at all past-dues surrounded Sarah, and Sidney was getting phone calls from certain parties asking, "When?" He went back to the books and became Scrooge. In a year or so they were again in the black.

Sarah was impressed and told him how wonderful it felt to be free and clear. Those words convinced Sidney that she'd learned life's what-fors. Again he proposed the household budget system on a cash basis.

"It's the only way," she said. He handed over a suitable amount and left for work knowing the by-laws were approved.

When he came home that evening, hanging over the sofa was a new $210 painting. Without a word he picked up the phone, made a call, and then went out to a friendly backroom where the boys dealt him in. He stayed until half past four when he cashed in a fifty-cent winner.

Thought for the day: *What a man wants is a sporting chance.*

The Shopper
Who Forgot What It Was Like

Do not lay up for yourselves treasures on earth.
—Matthew 6:19a

One Saturday morning a man named Harry set out to renew his acquaintances with grocery shopping after months of neglect, his time having been otherwise directed. It was good-scout time as his wife was preparing for a Sunday spread complete with good china and a linen cloth.

Harry walked into his friendly supermarket with a quick, easy gait, a broad smile, and a light heart. The easy gait went bye-bye near the meat counter; the broad smile never had a chance; and the weight his heart took on between the front door and the check-out stand was considerable.

He started tracking down a four-pound roast, which he found catalogued and filed midway up the meat counter. He was whistling a merry tune. On seeing the sum total of the selection of his choice the merry tune stopped on a high note.

Harry did an immediate it-couldn't-be-true, but contradicted himself when confronted with the prices per pound billboarded all along the counter. Some of these read "only." He did not know what this meant.

He noticed an unexpected craving for meat loaf and would have bought the hamburger, too, except his wife had said "roast." Domestic tranquility has its price also. The roast went into the cart.

Harry sneaked a glance at the price of cold cuts as he passed by, which was unfortunate. This produced an immediate vocal chord paralysis, complicated by severe coughing. An alert shopper administered the back-slapping rescue technique accompanied by, "Terrible, isn't it!" He did not reply. The left corner of his mouth twitched slightly.

He processed solemnly into the canned goods section for the meditation routine known among the laity as comparison shopping. With a can held in each hand, Harry noted their differences in price and size, and then lifted his face heavenward for wisdom and guidance. After meditating, one can went in the cart and the other back on the shelf. He repeated this ritual at designated intervals.

Once visions of happy children crossed his mind as he passed the candy stand. He remembered a former life when a nickel bought a candy bar for two. Right then in a carefree moment he gave a "Why not!" but the price stayed his hand. He compromised and slipped two packages of bubble gum with trading cards included into the cart.

Then it was check-out time. The checker pulled his cart forward. Harry stood transfixed as figures on the cash register did the slot machine whirl. After what seemed like forever there came grinding gears, ringing of bells, and a final figure that was awful. The checker with a loud cheery voice announced the grand sum to the whole house as though Harry had won first prize in a lottery.

He handed her a wad wondering what use there was in sweating away to lay up treasures in this world. He got no answer. Only six cents change, a friendly smile, and the enthusiastic instruction, "Have a good day!"

Thought for the day: *In giving advice, timing is everything.*

The Skinny Kid Who Trained to Be a Formidable Force

Rejoice, O young man, in your youth, . . . walk in the ways of your heart and in the sight of your eyes.
—Ecclesiastes 11:9a

In the gray house across the street lived a substandard physique who planned to show the big boys how. He'd do it on the high school football team.

When he stripped down he could tell he was not the sought-after material. He lacked natural padding. But he was undismayed. According to the success literature, will power and determination turned the world into a private oyster. Here his cup overflowed.

In June he was hard at it on a series of mail-order exercises calculated to transform him into a formidable force. These came at a ridiculously low price when one considered the splendid benefits plus a few cents postage and handling charges.

In no time at all he'd turn his 121-pound frame into the solid stuff that could dish it out. He was pure Spartan. He held up a halting hand to sweets and malts. Every meal was training table and when the time came he would outlast anything in a helmet.

Ever since when, his heart's desire was to be a gridiron marvel living by the roar of the crowd. He always had time to dream of pulling a spectacular that sports writers and fans simply could not get over. Being humble, he gave credit to the team, content in the knowledge that he'd proved determination and training counted more than brawn.

Finally, fall practice!

The physical specimen was ready to grab the inside lane while the 200-pounders were still gasping for breath. He did his calisthenics right in front of the coach so his superior condition would be noticed. He ended each session saying to himself, If I'm too pooped to drag, think how miserable those guys are. Down deep he felt compassion.

Soon it was serious practice with scrimmage drills. Compassion time was over; it was dog-eat-dog.

One day he entered the fray as a defensive back with a let-me-at-'em attitude. The first play was a hand-off to one who disregarded all training rules. He stayed out late at night, ate what he wanted, never did calisthenics unless the coach was looking. He was a disgrace and did not have the proper spirit to carry the school colors.

This poor excuse broke through the line heading straight for the physical specimen. Here was his chance to prove himself and to walk forever in the ways of his heart and the sight of his eyes. He maneuvered for a head-on tackle. His eyes widened, his heart pounded in anticipation. With a snarl of sadistic delight he spread his feet, lowered his head, and crushed into the 192-pound tub of lard. The lights went out.

When the formidable force opened his eys, the attending physician said two days bed rest would be quite in order.

Thought for the day: *There must be some to buy the tickets.*

The Mother Who Had Some Difficulty with Her Lot

*Lo, sons are a heritage from the Lord,
the fruit of the womb a reward.*
—Psalms 127:3

At the end of the block was a large brown house that was a proving ground for three members of the coming generation: male, ages four, five, and seven. The stairs and hallway were a combination fun house, demolition range, and destruction derby speedway complete with sound effects—all stops open, joined by a small black and white dog that jumped and barked loudly. When heard from a long distance this was known as "happy sounds."

Early each morning a grown man left this house. Word was that he was out chasing affluence. He was far back in the pack.

The coming generation called their overseer Mother. Some days she looked older than she was. She wanted some help-me from the boys to make their house a neat and tidy like those featured in women's magazines. Alone she could not keep abreast of the herd.

Her mornings began twenty-four hours late. She arose with yesterday's leftovers still in place. This was due to the heck-with-it attitude that snagged her when sleep finally floored the boys for the full count. The dinner dishes would keep 'til morning, and no company coming tonight, so let the scattered clothes be, ditto for the toys, dusting and vacuuming having already received a rescheduling.

Now she did crack a whip, but it could not be heard, the happy sounds being too loud. So one afternoon she did a learn-by-example touted by leading authorities. They cozy couched with her holding her favorite magazine, the boys nestled close. She showed them selected pictures, giving the moral about picking up their debris. This she said would give them a magazine-pictured home and wasn't that what they wanted. Before she took her third breath the youngest wanted cookies and milk, big brother kicked the five-year-old in the shins making him cry, and the dog crawled under the couch chewing an old beef bone.

The one called Mother said rude things and rushed to the kitchen to do something with her hands. She started a cake. This, she had read, released tension.

The coming generation built a drag strip down the stairs for their cars. Then they raced them to the bottom by sliding down the banister. All at once there was a loud out-of-the-ordinary sound that sent them on a hurry-up to the hospital emergency room. No breaks, but a sprained ankle, said the doctor.

In the rush, Mother forgot the cake, which was black and smoking when she returned. Then it was woe-is-me time. With her head on the table she wondered how this all came to pass and when it might be otherwise.

She remembered her single days as a full-timer at the answering service. While there she oft dreamed of having a large house, a chance to stay home and raise children, the rewards of her womb. Now her dreams were all around her, and so they would be for years to come. The thought choked her up, and she cried.

Thought for the day: *Many dreams lack details.*

The Congregation That Found a Need

*There appeared to them tongues as of fire, . . . resting on
each one of them.*

—Acts 2:3

Once there was a church in need of a new minister, the
previous one having reached the age when he could go out to
pasture and Nebuchadnezzar.

He did the farewell scene at a seventy-five-cents-a-plate
banquet in the church basement. The members barbershopped
"He's a Jolly Good Fellow," and gave him a new rod and reel
complete with instructions not to Huck Finn on Sunday
mornings.

Then he went his way, and the church did Article 7 of the
By-laws, this being a committee to seek and find.

The committee met in the church parlor on Wednesday
evening promptly at 7:30. The chairman was ready with coffee,
cookies, and a written agenda. It called for an opening prayer
followed by a pregame pep talk designed to impress that a picnic
this was not. He said they were charting the church's destiny.
Anathema was a fitting end for them if they did not rise properly
to the occasion!

He did such a superb job that four members were eager to
resign. The chairman backpaddled. What he really meant, he
said, was for them to do their best and trust the great
employment officer in the sky. The fainthearted stayed on to
consider the next item. What do we want in a minister?

There was splendid participation. Each member spoke with
the voice of authority. The scribe noted all items on the
blackboard until an image formed. They then agreed to
modifications since neither St. Paul nor St. Peter was available
for call.

Then it was cookie time, and while refreshing themselves, some remembered their former minister. "He was wise and kind. But we took advantage of him. We let him carry our bucket. Whenever he came to us for advice and counsel we said, 'You decide!' Except, of course, in financial matters."

One by one, the others said it was so. They resolved to no longer expect all to come from their minister. The laity would give direction to the church. These thoughts warmed their imaginations. Their enthusiasm grew hotter and hotter until their voices were like the rush of a mighty wind filling the room and tongues of fire seemed to sit on their heads. And each began to testify to the great things that were to come to them.

Word of this great moment spread through the congregation. There was a great Amen! Find us a minister who will work with such as we.

The search began.

While the search was yet in progress, a matter came before the congregation for consideration. Would they join with other churches, giving money and leadership to provide a neighborhood youth program?

The matter was discussed at great length. Then it was placed on the table until such time as their next minister could decide what to do about it.

Thought for the day: *A strong habit finds a way.*

The Justice of the Peace
Who Wanted a Wedding

He said to his daughters, "And where is he? Why have
you left the man? Call him, that he may eat bread."
                                        —Exodus 2:20

A justice of the peace had seven daughters whom the local
eligibles consistently passed over in their choice of life's
helpmates.

The father was past the stage of wondering why his wedlock
blessings had turned into marital liabilities. All he cared about
was marrying his daughters to acceptable young men. His
standards of acceptability grew increasingly liberal.

His desperation was a poorly kept secret. It leaked through his
eyes and oozed from his corrugated brow. Old-timers remembered that he used to smile, but as to just how long ago it had
been—that was a debating subject.

Town gossips and neighborhood sympathizers knew it as fact
that the daughters were on a twenty-four-hour standby alert as
back-up brides for every couple coming to be married. During
each wedding, one of the girls stood outside the ceremonial
room ready to substitute if the bride to be developed
second-thought falters.

Some folks didn't believe this story. Yet even they noticed the
family members didn't deny it. When the daughters heard it,
they just blushed. As for the J.P., he only chewed his cigar
harder, asked the dealer for two cards, then folded.

One day a stranger happened along as local pranksters started
fun-and-games at the sisters' expense. Jostling the girls, they
took their groceries, hid the cans, and played catch with the eggs
and canteloupe, while the sisters looked on helplessly. This had
become a regular Saturday afternoon custom.

The stranger routed these ne'er-do-wells, helped the ladies retrieve their groceries, and gave them the kind of personal attention that sent them running home to tell their father.

"Where is he!" shouted the J.P. "When a fish nibbles, you don't yank the bait. The first time you're treated like ladies, and you leave him! Now go get him, and bring him home for dinner!"

When they found Sir Galahad he was standing on a lonely street wondering about his future. He was alone in a strange town, unkempt, unemployed, broke, hungry, and with no place to sleep. He graciously accepted the sisters' invitation for free food and lodging.

After the meal, the girls cleared the table and the J.P had a long talk with the stranger to see if he met the standards of acceptability for a son-in-law. Near the end of the second cigar, the stranger agreed that if the J.P. set him up in a good business he would have all the necessary standards. They shook hands, and the J.P. was left with the feeling that it was safe for the girls to have at him.

A week later the stranger and the oldest daughter ran from the house under a shower of rice. As they drove off, the J.P. waved after them wearing the first big smile he'd had in years.

Thought for the day: *Some things aren't appreciated until they are gone.*

The Way-Out Minstrel
Who Sang One Too Many

And he [Samson] told her all his mind, and said to her, "A razor has never come upon my head; . . . If I be shaved, then my strength will leave me, and I shall become weak, and be like any other man."

—Judges 16:17

Once there was a minstrel who grew up without watching television, so he was ignorant of the benefits of soap and water. Also, he ran away from home before his first haircut in search of the simple life.

He took the poverty vow which forbade combs, razors, and change of clothes, found a black guitar with three chords, and roamed the streets singing mean songs about the Establishment. This gave him a high Nielsen with others who were thumbs down on conformity.

To hear him was sheer inspiration, for he sang with a message. And the message was that the reason all free and untrampled souls were so strong was that they were different from other men.

The great unwashed took note of their beards and hairdos and agreed that he sang with truth and insight. They named him "The One Who Tells It Like It Is" and commemorated his fame through the city backwashes.

Every night, The One went to a dark place that also served coffee. There he sang ballads while his friends listened and tasted life close to the bone. They talked of the Philistines slaving in the marketplaces and worshiping false gods; they laughed cruelly at the world and then basked in the warm glow of their own virtue.

One night, while they lolled on their backsides as usual, The

One rose to sing a touching lament. It was of a young girl whose father dragged her from the True Life back into middle-class slavery. There she lived out her days a prisoner of the system.

Near the end of the sixth chorus, he accidentally stepped on a banana peel. Whereupon he tried touching the ceiling with both feet simultaneously while cracking his head against the table. This gave his conscious mind an extended rest and earned him red lights and siren all the way to the hospital.

The doctor gave him a close pruning so he could take four stitches in his head, then left him to a Florence Nightingale. She was a crusader for cleanliness and a warrior against contamination. She shaved off his beard, bathed him with antiseptic soap, wrapped him in a clean gown, tucked him neatly between two sterile sheets, and left him to awake at his leisure.

In the meantime his friends came to do vigil during this, his time of suffering and need. But when they saw him, their sense of pity gave way to horrified disbelief. He was like any other man: clean, common, with his strength gone from him.

They turned away and left, having lost all faith in him.

Thought for the day: *Backsliding is not for saviors.*

The Woman Who Made an Unsettling Discovery

If salt has lost its taste, how shall its saltness be restored?
*—Matthew 5:13*b

There was a woman who was a shoo-in for life's checkered flag, laurel wreath and all. She was talent and personality, making her envy number one in the ladies' set and other places of circulation. Filling her home with isn't-it-clever arrangements from bits of unlikelies was a snap. And she turned out home sewn you-wouldn't-believes for herself and children, with time left over to go out with her husband and be a handsome couple. The smile in her "tell me about yourself" put strangers at ease, giving her a high-up on all invitation lists.

While cruising along at high speed, she developed early symptoms of the middle years. She looked back at where she'd come from and asked some what-it-all-meant questions, a subject filled with pondering possibilities. This forced her into a pit stop to work things out, which turned into a long delay, being one who did not like to leave blanks on test papers.

She stored her talents on the top shelf so as to be unencumbered while searching for answers. Home held together by the marvels of frozen TV dinners which the other half of the handsome couple threw into the oven, she being nowhere around while exchanging isn't-it-awfuls with friends who were in likewise condition. Or she was reading a magazine article by one of her kind who had hunches that sounded good because of the impressive letters following the author's name.

Research of such in-depth quality was sure to turn up something, which it did. It came to her all at once. Her salt of life had lost its taste, and she did not know how to restore its saltiness. A fact she passed on to hubby who did a how-much-longer routine, exclamation marks included. It was then boo-hoo time, and "You really don't understand." Then she colored herself "unfulfilled."

This sent him for a long walk in the night air and her to a twelve-week group adventure with one who had found a road to fulfillment and was willing to have company for a fee that commanded respect—easy monthly payments, 10 percent higher.

The fee entitled her to one psychological interior design job and a personalized set of practical applications for getting life salty again. These marvels would be accomplished by "freeing up, self-expression, discovering potential" done in accordance with sure-fire methods that change black and white humdrums into living color sound-tracked with "Why didn't I know of this before!"

At the end of her twelve-week sentence it was clear that home was not a complete outlet for one as talented as she. According to her detailed, personalized practicals, high priority was a commercial setting: a special place to combine her easy way with people and her great aesthetic abilities. A combo like this was certain to enrich her and those she touched, besides bringing in the long green.

It was heartwarming to watch the new design job leave the pit and take to the road again. When last seen she was doing a part-time, selling framed pictures in a five-and-dime.

Thought for the day: *It's where you find it.*

The Parks Department
That Made Things Better than They Were

And they . . . rejoiced in the works of their hands.
—Acts 7:41

There was once a certain city in favor of children by a five-to-three majority. This gave the parks department a special interest in frolicking youth and where to put them.

Those in charge of this round-up knew the importance of proper play as per Recreation Course No. 352, "Playground Theory and Design," or its equivalent with collateral reading as approved. Being academically grounded, they could talk about "muscle building," "socialization," and other words important to the future of growing children. Each understood that a child deprived of such playground wonders was forever scarred, the results too tragic to discuss, except, of course, at budget hearings and other influential gatherings.

One day departmental orders directed heavy equipment and men to use it to a vacant spot that backed into a hillside nature had stopped maintaining. It was where neighborhood children did leisure time, learning play by the self-taught method. Meaning it was common, ordinary, and without planned direction.

They turned themselves into what some called "a sight" by rolling over and over on the hill from the top to the bottom where the tall weeds grew—which was really a jungle for stalking wild game, a most dangerous adventure, especially with cannibals nearby. On one safari they found an old bone—a sure sign of an ancient burial ground with rich hidden treasures. They would be digging yet, but it was soon lunchtime and home. Then it rained, so they had sit-down slide races on the muddy hillside, the winner receiving a large helping of satisfaction. Seeing children happy like this made many mothers cry.

Such an unkept place was sure to have an old wooden crate, which it did. Being too big and heavy to move, the self-taughts turned it into a combination clubhouse, fort, castle, hideout, and headquarters for telling magnificent secrets.

After the heavy equipment made the scene it was no time at all before it was not the same place. It became a real playground properly designed from surveys, charts, and expert opinion. The hillside looked so pretty nature took an interest again.

Also, there were swings, slides, ladders and bars, a hard surface for bounce ball, and other great games. And for the mere cost of a living wage there came one who specialized in exercising childrens' imaginations by the arts-and-crafts method. All who saw the transformation gave it an isn't-it-wonderful and the parks department rejoiced in the work of their hands.

The children were so excited it took them three days to check out the equipment and make something nifty from the art supplies. The rest of the summer they went about the neighborhood feeling bored because there was nothing to do.

Thought for the day: *Grown-ups take the fun out of play.*

The Poor Man
and the Generous Photographer

You always have the poor with you.
—Matthew 26:11a

There was once a family of lesser means who called a certain house "home" because they had no place else to go.

It had a tired foundation and matching roof line. In a good year the shingles shed 65 percent of the rainfall. The paint had parted company with the siding; this brought out the wood's natural quality. The walls were well cracked, providing excellent ventilation on cold days.

The plumbing was expiring of old age, and draining the kitchen sink paralyzed it with exhaustion. This gave the children no chance for a who's who with the dishwashing.

The county assessor listed the house as an "improved dwelling" while the landlord called it "income property." But being a proper sort, he did not charge extra for any wildlife nesting in the walls.

The head of this household was a seasonal pulling down $1.50 an hour, now and then. When he got it, it was family celebration complete with boiled potatoes and fried dough. Then early to bed, because tomorrow was another day filled with the usual opportunities.

One day when he was between jobs the head of this improved dwelling leaned against the front door away from the flies. He had nothing on his mind and noticed that his stomach was in a likewise condition.

While wondering what to do about it, there happened along a camera-carrying person in search of a likely subject. His specialty was "human interest," as it was called in the trade. He was self-trained in the art of finding a this-is-it scene in unlikely places.

He saw the monarch and his castle and knew right away he had a you-always-have-the-poor-with-you shot. He needed only to fit it into his viewfinder.

So he walked up and made the necessary introductions, giving the pitch about the face with character that told a story which should be on film. And no, he wasn't collecting information for the welfare department. Just to prove it he was willing to go as high as ten dollars for the opportunity.

Right then it became a what'll-I-do conversation with the photographer giving the directions and the man doing the listening.

He had him take the time-on-my-hands pose by sitting on the porch rail, being careful to frame in the many distinctive qualities of the house. Then he set up reflectors to get the sun working on his side casting shadows in the proper places. Next came the camera angle that separated him from the amateurs. Then some calculations with gadgets specially designed for such occasions. He did the final countdown on his camera, snapped off several black and whites, paid the ten dollars, and left.

He titled the finished print Shadows of Poverty, then entered it in an annual photo contest, and won a five-hundred-dollar first prize.

Thought for the day: *Looking at it and living in it aren't the same.*

The Young Man
Who Was Faithful to the End

He who is faithful in a very little is faithful also in much.
*—Luke 16:10*a

Once there was a certain young man, seventeen years old to be exact, who wanted to learn an applied manual skill to be properly prepared for life's eventualities. He chose karate.

He went to a gym where the skill was known to be taught in a superior way. First, they extracted a superior fee, and then attired him in the approved dress, it being patterned after white canvas pajamas with full legs, ballooned sleeves, and a plunging neckline. This wardrobe could be accented with a beautiful belt colored ferocious to those who knew the code. Hard work and practice were all that would be needed.

He made a silent vow to be diligent—reminding himself that by being faithful in the very little, he would be faithful in much. Immediately he became a three-nights-a-weeker at the gym with overtime on Saturday morning and reading karate literature in between. Soon he knew the proper care and handling of the adversary's vital spots, complete with those chops and kicks that distinguished between sending him to the orthopedic surgeon or bringing an undertaker on the run. All done with a special-effects yell that would make a dog do a turn-tail.

The superior instruction emphasized the high ideal of respect and honor for one's opponent, by means of bowing one to another before engaging in simulated mayhem. Having thus paid their respects, the students could go at it hand and foot with a clear conscience.

Now the faithful one's resoluteness was beginning to tell. He could break a board with a single blow from his hand. In combat contests he outscored opponents in city-wides. Trophies began to adorn his room and the color of his belt grew more ferocious.

One day he and his sister, who was something to look at, were walking along an isolated stretch when met by an uncouth who made certain remarks about the sister to which the brother took offense. He decided an apology was in order or else the breaker of boards would take matters into his own hands. The outcome of such an event would be too horrible to imagine.

He stopped the uncouth and announced what was expected of him in a voice calculated to command respect. While issuing these clear, straightforward instructions he felt the uncouth's fist sink deep into his stomach. Next, something caught him under the chin, lifting him off his feet, then he fell to the ground from several directions at once.

When the stars stopped circling, his sister—holding his head—asked why in the world he'd not used some karate on the bully.

"I was going to," he said, "but he never bowed!"

Thought for the day: *Do not stand on ceremony when meeting strangers.*